WITHDRAWN

TRUCKS

Meg Greve
J. Jean Robertson

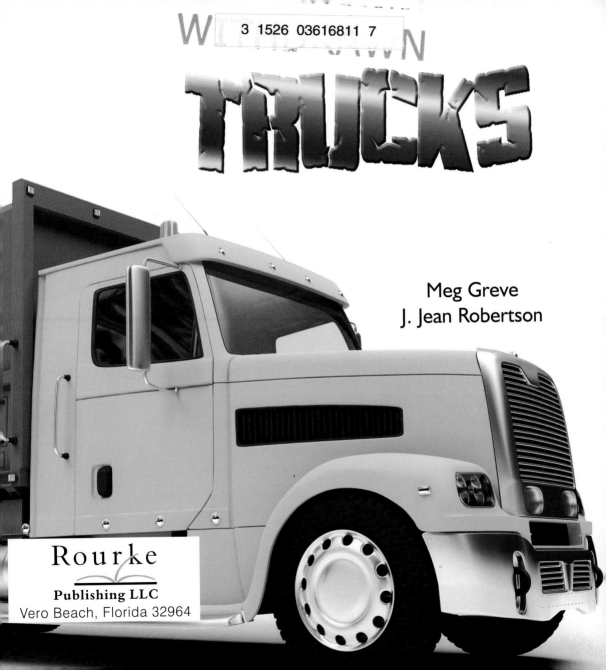

Rourke
Publishing LLC
Vero Beach, Florida 32964

www.rourkepublishing.com

PHOTO CREDITS: © Ickncg: Cover, Title Page; © Todd Harrison: page 3 top; © Brian Sullivan: page 3 bottom; © Igor Lubnevskiy: page 4, 5, 6, 9; © Jon Patton: page 7, 20, 21; © Skip O'Donnell: page 8; © Christophe Testi: page 10; © Rob Fox: page 11; © Andrew Penner: page 12; © Julio de la Higuera: page 13; © Christine Balderas: page 14; © Brian Sullivan: page 15; © Stan Rohrer: page 16; © Matt Richard: page 17; © Terry North: page 18, 19;

Editor: Jeanne Sturm

Cover design by: Nicola Stratford: bdpublishing.com

Interior design by: Renee Brady

Library of Congress Cataloging-in-Publication Data

Greve, Meg.
  Trucks / Meg Greve and J. Jean Robertson.
    p. cm. -- (My first discovery library)
  ISBN 978-1-60472-527-8
  1. Trucks--Juvenile literature. I. Robertson, J. Jean. II. Title.
  TL230.15.G7452 2009
  629.224--dc22
                          2008025165

Printed in the USA

CG/CG

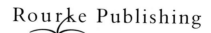

Rourke Publishing

www.rourkepublishing.com – rourke@rourkepublishing.com
Post Office Box 3328, Vero Beach, FL 32964

Do you like trucks?

Eighteen-wheelers move very fast.

It's fun to watch them whizzing past.

Trucks roll down the road on giant wheels,

FOOD MART

6

bringing us
milk and food
for our meals.

7

Emergency trucks help us save each other.

PARAMEDIC

They quickly arrive, one after another.

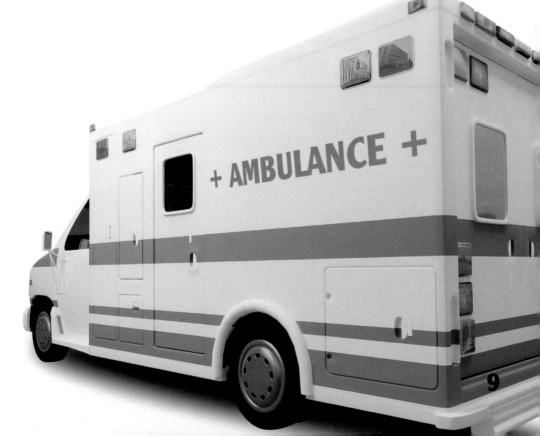

+ AMBULANCE +

9

Fire trucks are both large and small.

When there is a fire,
we welcome them all.

Flatbed trucks haul things down our roads,

but cranes move up, up, up with their loads.

13

A tow truck is made to lift a big car.

TOWING

A pick-up
may travel
near and far.

Dump trucks carry heavy loads.

Some act as snowplows, clearing our roads.

Log trucks may carry just one huge tree,

or be piled with small ones, as you can see.

A truck might be a yellow bus,

carrying children, just like us!

Glossary

cranes (KRANEZ): Cranes are machines with long arms to lift heavy loads high. Some cranes are part of a big truck; others are not.

dump trucks (DUHMP TRUHKS): Dump trucks are used to carry big loads. They bring sand, gravel, or dirt to a construction crew. Dump trucks are made so the back part can lift up and empty its load.

eighteen-wheelers (ate-teen WEEL-urz): Eighteen-wheelers are trucks with cabs and trailers. They have 18 wheels, with 6 on the cab and 12 on the trailer. Eighteen-wheelers carry lots of things. They bring our favorite foods to the grocery store, and toys to the toy store.

emergency trucks (i-MUR-juhn-see TRUHKS): Emergency trucks carry equipment and people to take care of problems. 9-1-1 is the emergency number to call if an emergency truck is needed.

fire trucks (FIRE TRUHKS): Fire trucks are the emergency trucks which carry firemen and equipment to fight fires. Fire trucks may carry ladders, water, fire hoses, axes, and fire extinguishers.

log trucks (LOG TRUHKS): Log trucks are trucks made specially to carry logs. Logs are tree trunks which have fallen or have been cut down.

tow trucks (TOH TRUHKS): Tow trucks are used to move cars and trucks that can not be driven. They are very strong. Sometimes tow trucks move cars and trucks by pulling them, and sometimes they move them by carrying them. **23**

Index

Further Reading

Bingham, Caroline. *Fire Truck.* DK Publishers, Inc., 2006.

Bingham, Caroline. *Big Book of Trucks.* DK Publishers, Inc., 2000.

Priddy, Roger. *My Big Truck Book.* Priddy Books, 2002.

Scarry, Richard. *Cars and Trucks and Things That Go.* Random House Children's Books, 1998.

Websites

www.dos.state.ny.us/kidsroom/firesafe/trucks.html

About the Authors

Meg Greve, an elementary teacher, lives in Chicago with her family. Currently, she is taking some time to enjoy being a mother and reading to her own children every day.

J. Jean Robertson, also known as Bushka to her grandchildren and many other kids, loves to read, travel, and write books for children. After teaching for many years, she retired to San Antonio, Florida where she lives with her husband.